S<small>UNDROPS</small> <small>ON</small> L<small>IFE</small>

V<small>OLUME</small> 2

W<small>ORRY</small>

F<small>AITH</small>

W<small>ISDOM</small>

www.patrickinspires.com

Patrick McBride

Copyright 2003-2009 Patrick J. McBride
All Rights Reserved

All Rights Reserved. No part of this book may be reproduced in any form or by any electronic or mechanical means, including information storage and retrieval systems, without permission in writing from the publisher, except by a reviewer, who may quote brief passages in a review. Any members of educational institutions wishing to photocopy part or all of the work for classroom use, or publishers who would like to obtain permission to include the work or any part thereof in an anthology, should send their inquiries to inquiries@patrickinspires.com.

ISBN 978-0-615-32478-4

Produced in the United States
First Printing November 2009
Published by Allistar Publishing

Dedication

To Mother

Acknowledgments

Sundrops on Life would be nothing more than scattered thoughts if it were not for some amazing people that the Director placed in my life. First and foremost, it is my angel Jane, the embodiment of all that is beautiful in this world. My family has been a fountain of love that I never can get enough of in this lifetime. Elaine Brzezinski for starting the idea of books of Sundrops. Dana Withers for her input and meticulous proofreading. And last, but certainly not least, Amma, my guide and teacher.

The longer paragraphs in this book come from talks that I have given on Sunday mornings to some amazing people whom I love. Each ends with a question, as do most days in my life.

Introduction

I have been very fortunate in my life to have been a failure at many things, to have made many mistakes — both gigantic and tiny, and to be surrounded by people who constantly upset me. I have also been very fortunate in my life to have been a success at many things, to have done many things right, and to be surrounded by people that make my heart sing.

You see, all of life — the good, the bad, and the ugly — is amazingly fortunate. Every mistake, every wrong action is a lesson to ourselves and those around us. Every success, every right action is a cause for celebration and an affirmation that life says, "Yes!" as often as it says, "No!" … and both are absolutely necessary. Everything that happens to us fills another chapter in the wonderful book of life. We will all make a contribution to it with the years of our life. Life doesn't judge, it merely records it.

What movie would be entertaining to watch if there were not both tears and laughter, as well as those moments when you had no clue about what was happening? The play of life follows God's script for the greatest of all directors and knows exactly what the perfect part is for us.

If we complain about our costume, character, or lines, it will make our part that much harder to enjoy. But, regardless, we will play our part.

Someday, in some far off nirvana, we may get to sit back and watch the whole play and we will see that each one of us played a pivotal role.

Until then, try not to **worry**, have *faith* in the Director, harvest the **wisdom** from your mistakes, and enjoy this heavenly production.

Contents

Worry

Stress does not come from having too much on your plate. Stress comes from labeling too many of those things as very important.

The present moment, by itself, cannot create fear. In order to create fear, we first have to imagine a dark future and then convince ourselves that it's probably a certainty.

Today is proof positive that you were seriously mistaken each and every time you said that you couldn't go on. Odds are that, if you ever say it again, it won't be true then either.

Replaying a problem over and over again in your mind should never be confused with actually doing something about it.

Focusing on your problems uncovers more problems, but focusing on helping someone else with their problems always diminishes yours.

Better to be shot by a dozen arrows than to be filled with doubt, because it is possible that the arrows might not completely destroy your life.

It is not the problem that causes the madness. It is the undisciplined mind incessantly clamoring for a reason or an answer.

You can train your fears to be your constant companion by feeding them with your attention every time they come around.

A stadium could not hold all of our
current worries, but a thimble could easily
hold all of our past worries.

If a weed sprouts in our garden, it would grow quite
big if we only studied it. Cast it aside every time it
surfaces and be done with it, and it becomes
compost for what we really want to grow.

Sadness is less a result of what is
going on and more a result of having
had different expectations.

The experience of driving a car would be filled with
anxiety if you were to think about every mechanical
process and how it might fail. Life is no different.

We look at our future problems and feel
hopeless because we do not trust that with
the problems of the future will also come the tools
and solutions of the future.

Up to this point you have adapted to every
single difficulty that life has thrown at you.
In order to properly worry, you must try very
hard to forget this fact.

When you hit a rough patch of road while driving,
your awareness goes to its highest level. Now you
know why we have periods of difficulty in our lives.

Of all the connections available to us, worry is the
weakest. It makes us feel like we are connected to
others, but bestows no benefits upon us or them.

You can easily coexist with any and
all of your emotions if you remember to
remain their master.

Some problems in our life were never meant to be
solved. They are in our lives to teach us that life
goes on, even amidst adversity.

The question is not whether you can make it
through this, but whether you can stop rejecting
the help that will make it easier.

Nothing sits in the middle of your brain,
refusing to budge, more defiantly than
money worries. Only a detailed plan and
rampant optimism will dislodge it.

You can handle everything that happens to you but only Superman could handle everything that you think might happen to you.

Trying to read a newspaper that is being blown by the wind is the same as trying to find a loving thought in an agitated mind. Calm the mind first.

When we owe, we worry about getting even. When we get even, we worry about getting ahead. When we get ahead, we worry about losing it all. Worry is the cause of unhappiness; not the ebb and flow of our money.

When a storm approaches, cast off your lines and sail around it or fight through it. More boats are damaged by the dock that they held to for security than the open sea.

Our fears and our anxieties and our irritations are more of a product of our fatigue than of anything truly wrong. Be conscious of your breath and learn to relax.

To the mind that is filled with worry and fear comes abundant blessings, but finding no room, they move on.

It is in the jumping over doubts that we gain the strength to surmount obstacles.

In order to properly worry, you must first disregard any history of making it through a crisis. Secondly, you must close your eyes and pretend that you are alone.

What if I stuffed your pockets with hundred dollar bills and sent you out into the world, but for the entire time you were out, you never once reached into your pockets. You slept in doorways, you begged for food and drink from others, and you spent most of your time cursing your lot in life.

Do you know anyone who is rich with many, many blessings, and yet acts as if they have nothing?

One of the greatest questions we can ask ourselves has nothing to do with the meaning of life. It is simply: Are things really that bad or am I just tired?

The solution to ridding ourselves of an unwanted, obsessive thought is not just by choosing any good thought. You must replace it with a good thought of the same magnitude.

Today is tinted with worry because yesterday, when today was a tomorrow, we painted it so. Never be afraid of what you see ahead of you. More often than not, it's just a two-dimensional picture painted with your fears and you can walk right through without a scratch.

The weight of the world drops off the back of the person who decides to stand up and hold their head high.

You have your choice of miracles and colors and music and blessings to set your mood and yet you choose a sliver of news to affirm that life is depressing.

When a crisis happens, you will live or die. If you die, you die. If you live, you will adapt. You were made to die but once. You were made to adapt infinitely.

Worry can do many things with the glaring exception of finding a solution. Nothing in nature seeks its own demise; a solution would mean the demise of worry.

We magnify our problems in order to see them better and then we forget that we have magnified them and become fearful of their size.

The darkness can only frighten those who choose to hide the light that they carry.

Shed thy worries with the receding darkness each morn and thy days shall always dawn with a light that guides thee gently towards happiness.

Not feeling well or not having enough money are not acceptable excuses for unhappiness unless everyone who is well and has money is deliriously happy.

When we have something to celebrate, somehow we always find a way to put negativity aside.

Fear stands naked and vulnerable
all by itself but clothe it in drama and it is
fit to vanquish all.

Worries are the sandbags on the side
of hot air balloons. The more you release,
the higher you fly.

Worries taunt us from a day that has not come and
we voluntarily destroy the peace of this moment by
imagining that it has.

If we see life as capricious, we will always be on
guard for what's next. But if we see life as God's
creation, we will drop our guard and say a loud,
"Yes!" to whatever comes next.

You wouldn't give up walking in the woods for fear of bumping into a tree, so why give up your dreams for fear of bumping into a failure?

Thoughts that disturb your harmony must be sent on their way. Simply say, "Go in peace" each time the thought enters your consciousness and refuse it more attention.

When life feels out of control, our tendency is to run around and quickly find an answer, but the answers, as always, are only found in stillness.

Train yourself to have a positive expectancy when you have an inclination that something is going to happen.

How easily a very biased review of our life and accomplishments masquerades as the truth when we are in a negative frame of mind.

How fortunate are those whose problems in life are so great that they start a quest for the source of inner strength.

If we could chant the words of love as often as we worry, there would soon be no worry.

The seasons, the laws of nature, and the universe all operate in a Divine order, and yet we think that our problems are somehow outside of all that.

It's not that we can't make a decision. It's that
we are afraid of upsetting our happiness and
comfort with what we decide.

Our anxiety is doubled when what gave us balance
last time doesn't work this time. Be quiet, stop
searching for yesterday's prayer, and listen for
today's.

Imagine the very worst that can happen
and figure out how you would cope,
and having accomplished that, live.

We could easily handle most things in life if we
didn't constantly worry that whatever was
happening was leading to something worse.

Troubles are part of every life. One-third of our sadness is from our troubles but two-thirds of our sadness is from worrying over our troubles.

Carrying a feather is easy, but encase it in cement and it becomes a chore. Your problems can be handled with time, but encase them in drama and they become too heavy to bear.

The rarest of thoughts is the thought to lighten up. When we are happy, it is unnecessary and when we are down, it is hidden by the darkness.

Endlessly looking for a reason why something happened is the best way to stay firmly attached to what happened.

When we feel out of balance, we try with all of our resources to get back to where we were. What if life is trying to take us forward to a better place?

To go out into the storm in search of peace is futile. When a storm is raging, peace can only be found inside.

You would not go into an apple orchard and eat the weeds, so why would you go into your day and feast on worries?

Instead of being a source of strength when someone whom we care about is in a crisis, we waste a great deal of energy in becoming frantic and terribly upset to show that we care.

Your connection to those you love
is not strengthened by worry.

Running from any fearful thought empowers
it and exhausts us. This will continue
until we turn, face it, and embrace it.

A positive outlook is hard to nurture
when we foolishly believe that our good luck
is somehow a random act of fortune
but our bad luck has been earned.

No matter what is bothering you,
there is a place inside of you where everything
is all right. "Take It Easy" is the name of the
street that gets you there.

Most people visit Upset Town once in a while
but only fools rent a room there.

If you went to the most beautiful place on earth
and thought about negative things, it would not
seem like paradise. Where you are right now is
equally affected.

If we see each crisis as a problem, we are closed by
our resistance; but if we see each crisis as an
adventure, our very openness allows the solution to
come rushing in.

Worry takes control by falsely promising a
solution if we consider enough negative outcomes.
To regain control we must shout "enough!"
because worry never will.

You dig a beautiful hole and you fill it with clear, clean water and you decorate around the edges and you think that it is done. But soon, the water turns swampy and attracts unwanted things. All that does not flow stagnates. Water, ideas, plans, relationships, and others.

What started out great in your life but is now stagnating? What can you do to start it flowing?

When change shows up completely unannounced, you can throw yourself against the door to keep it out only to watch it drop through the ceiling, or you can put on your favorite music and dance with it.

A detour doesn't mean that you stop driving. It just means that you drive on a different road to get to the same place. It would be ridiculous to think that it meant failure.

Always have one beautiful thought that you can picture in your mind and practice replacing any thought with that one. With practice, no negative thought will ever be able to take over.

Don't let your problems define who you are. You are always light and love and perfection and you just happen to have a problem or two.

Most of us who have danced with madness more than once or twice know that no matter how frightening the music, it's still just a dance.

One of the best reasons to exercise is so that every little ache and pain will be attributed to the exercise you did rather than some dark and dire worry.

The headlights of your car only illuminate a hundred yards or so in front of you and yet you feel perfectly safe driving all night. Don't fear the darkness, just focus on the light ahead.

Fear is a leash that tethers you
to what you don't want.

Whether you dance under the sword of
Damocles or you sit still in fear makes
no difference to the sword.

Much of what we call luck is Heaven's reward
for those who find the courage to
walk past the shadows.

When everything seems to be going wrong, the first
problem to deal with is our misperception that
everything is going wrong.

Every crisis has two outstanding benefits.
It forces us to grow stronger to survive and it
gives hope to those who are watching.

Keep complaining and you will keep alive
whatever you are complaining about.
Search for solutions without complaining
and it will finally begin to change.

Thinking is the prelude to creating unless the
thinking includes worrying. In that case, thinking
just continues in a loop without ever creating.

The changes that loom in front of you are the
doorway to the happiest time of your life. Disregard
the paintings of monsters on the door. Your fears
just arrived before you did.

A feeling of uncomfortableness before you do
something you have never done before is nothing
more than a tight lid on a brand new jar of courage.

You can worry about the rain or you can stop worrying and carry an umbrella. If you do not have an umbrella, worry will not provide one.

Strong people see past the fear of change and become successful. Weak people misinterpret the fear as a sign that it shouldn't be undertaken.

No one can see clearly around the corner to tomorrow. Always trust that when you wake up tomorrow morning, having turned that corner, you'll be ready.

How scary would the dark woods be if they were flooded with lights and music? How dark would your mood be if you did the same?

From a distance, mountains look like the end of the
road, but up close, it is easy to see the tunnel
through them. Don't prejudge your problems.

Fear can be born in the belly or in the brain.
But no matter where its origin, it needs you
to think "what if" in order for it to grow.

Affairs of the world are the place that the
pessimist can always find the sorrow that's
lacking in a personal life.

If you had laughed instead of worried in the past,
you might still have come to the same place, but
you wouldn't be so tired.

You have great opportunities surrounding you right now. They are hidden by your worrying and by your complaining. In twenty years, today's worries will be seen as they truly are — miniscule. The missed opportunities will loom as large as ever. Don't dig for clarity. Stop stirring up the mud with your worries. Allow them to settle for just a little while, and then the clarity you seek will be there.

In twenty years, you are going to be very upset or very proud of what you did this month. Which will it be?

If a hundred pebbles were coming towards you, you would duck. But if a hundred thoughts are coming at you, you try to handle them all.

While we continue to search for the why, the thing we wish to be rid of will never die.

When we walk into a dark room, we don't look for the cause of the darkness, we simply make finding a way to light up the room our number one priority.

One thing goes right in our day and we smile thankfully. One thing goes wrong in our day and we brace ourselves for the avalanche of misery that is surely portends.

Fear makes us worry. Worry causes us to react with tension. We try to relax and get rid of the tension and when we can't, we fear that there really is something wrong. Very silly.

When we put energy into something specific or something general, the specific is always easier to create. Our wishes are usually general and our problems are usually quite specific.

Nothing is more sad than taking a little game like "what's wrong with this picture" and making it an outlook on life.

It is not some big, evil monster that keeps us from stepping out of our box. It is the fear that even a tiny bit of regret might show up if we do.

No one fears the lights going out in the daytime because there is a greater source of light available. Whatever darkness befalls you, keep the shades up.

When the crying and the sighing stop, it is time to begin the changes that came to mind right before the crying and the sighing stopped.

Every single night that you thought would never end, did. Whatever darkness has you believing that it will never end is lying.

The most beautiful fireworks display is only just frightening sounds to those who close their eyes. Open your eyes and that which you fear is transformed.

When you reach that point where there is no place left to turn, it doesn't mean it's over. On the contrary, it means that you finally have the strength to face everything.

Safety brings security. Security brings boredom. Boredom brings exploration. Exploration brings unknowns. Unknowns bring a need for security. Enjoy, don't criticize the cycle.

You can either do something about it or you can worry about it. If you choose to worry, go ahead but don't deceive yourself into believing that you are doing something.

Mental strength is not accessed by tensing up for that is merely physical strength. Mental strength is only fully accessed by relaxing. A tense mind produces only tension and not solutions.

A beautiful blue sky with a few clouds is called a beautiful day and not a cloudy one. Why then can we not see the beauty in a life with a few problems?

Every little ache and pain does not need a cure because most are like dark clouds that pass without rain, but stay under that cloud as it moves and you will eventually get wet.

We are so adverse to change that the moment we feel out of sorts, even though there are many possible causes, we blame it on whatever change we made recently.

The commonality of all of your good days is that you were not worrying.

If they could, most people would banish frustration
from their life unaware that it is the only medium
where patience can grow.

'Tis thoughts of joy or thoughts of worry that steer
this ship we've been given. One leads to sunny isles
and the other to submersion.

Humor does not detach one from their problems,
but it does allow a person to stand on top of their
problems rather than being crushed beneath them.

The greatest thief on earth is not the person with a
gun, it's the problem that was worried about but
never happened. It stole part of a life of joy.

There has never been a time and there will never be a time when you have no problems, but hopefully, there may come a time when you will consider your problems insignificant.

It is only after being upset so many times that you start to catch a glimpse of a part of you that is never affected. When you can get in touch with that part, you have come home.

Getting upset because of an unexpected change in our life, we expend so much energy complaining about the change that we have little energy to actually deal with it.

Like an underwater cave full of jewels that can only be reached by diving deep, sometimes our depression is merely the deep dive to all of our awareness.

The fear of what might happen darkens the approach of both the good and the bad. If nothing bad happens, the fear will still make it seem like there is very little good around.

Many times in the past we have been incorrect about what was wrong with us but, unbelievably, it never stops us from panicking about our latest self diagnosis.

The successful gardener does not spend time looking for the source of a weed. He plucks it out, throws it away, and tends to the flowers.

We worry because we need a stimulating way to stay focused on a problem. That always makes it difficult to find a peaceful solution.

We watch out for fire and sharp things and germs, and yet, we pay no attention to the most dangerous thing of all – doubt. We doubt that we are loved. We doubt that everything will work out. When Jesus called to Peter to walk on the water with him, he was fine until he doubted he could do it because of the turbulence - and then he started to sink.

If you feel like you are sinking – what doubt can you get rid of?

If you send a good hearty laugh at your stack of
troubles and problems, the few that remain will be
only ones that you need to work on.

Negative thoughts can walk in unannounced but
they will only stay if you feed them.

When someone is in dire straits our first inclination
is to worry about them, but no one has ever been
helped by standing in a shower of someone else's
worrying.

When you are feeling overwhelmed, pray not for
the strength to handle it all but for the clarity to
know what really needs your attention and what
doesn't.

If you are steeped in a negative mood because of a
problem it will be difficult to find a positive solution.
All solutions reside within the confines of a positive
expectancy.

When the sun inevitably shines after a storm,
it is so much more appreciated than it was
before the storm. Focus on the sunshine
and not on the storm that past.

Although it may seem ominous and threatening, no
cloud can turn a day exactly into night and no
problem can block all of the light.

You can only blame Heaven for your
troubles if you wait long enough to see that
no good came from them.

We perceive life as difficult because we acknowledge our blessings for a moment, but we recall and study our worries for hours.

What would be the worth of learning all that you are spiritually learning if you don't have an exasperating problem to use it on every now and then?

Worrying is the delusion of being concerned or involved or connected. Worrying is not a solution. Worrying is not even the pathway to a solution. Worrying is impotent drama. Choose faith instead.

Because we are so caring and loving, we justify our worrying unaware that worrying soon takes the place of caring and loving.

Do not be frightened if your path seems to appear
dark when you look forward. The light always
travels with you, never ahead of you.

Some changes we can see coming. Fear them and
you will begin to suffer before they ever reach you.
Instead, have the faith to love them as Divinely sent
and you will trade fear for joyous expectancy.

The feeling that everything is going wrong
begins to change the moment you start to
focus on anything that is going right.

Worry causes more sickness than all
the germs in the world. Forget anti-bacterial
and work on anti-worry.

How we laugh at the thought of monsters under our bed, but how seriously we take the thought of being without help in the future.

If yesterday was difficult, then today should be filled with gratitude that it has past. Instead today is filled with so many retellings of yesterday that it is bound to duplicate.

Rant and rave and jump up and down and still the facts remain unchanged. Accept the facts or accept that you can't handle them but don't make believe they are different than they are.

If you are anxious and worried about yourself or another person, it is of no help at all. Negatives cannot give positive results.

A caterpillar doesn't die when he becomes a butterfly. He just goes through a change that is worthy of getting wings.

Negative happenings are not a sign that something is wrong with your life. Life is a mix of positive and negative like a great shower is a mix of hot and cold.

If the time and energy spent in worrying were actually spent in working and planning, there would be less to worry about.

The rainbow doesn't say that there will be no more storms. It merely says stop thinking about the storm for a moment and focus on something beautiful.

Each time that you feel upset or angry you probably have a very good reason for it. You keep recalling this incident so that it becomes stronger and worthy of your anger. Pretty soon you are really upset. You have a choice and you have voluntarily made your upset more important than your own joy and happiness.

Is it worth it?

When it seems like you can't go on, it's time to rest
and reconsider the path that you are on. It doesn't
mean that you're finished walking.

We do not prepare all day for the night
unless we are scared of it. Do not prepare for
every single day of the future; rather, learn to deal
with your fear of it.

Every regret is a doorway to a lesson.
We rarely acknowledge the lesson, but we
constantly replay the regret and wonder why we
can't move through it.

Fear is only a picture of a cliff right in front of you.
Walking through the picture is the way to get to
where you want to go.

You were not given strength to help you deal with loss. You were given strength to be able to look through the loss and see it as a change.

Repeating and rehashing the problem is the best way to keep from having to implement a solution.

Change is our constant companion and only those who ignore it are frightened when it is in front of us again.

Trying to solve our problems without first finding out how to bring peace to our minds is like trying to shoot pool with a snake instead of a cue.

A person is not weak because they
experience fear. A person is weak because
they don't expect to feel fear.

If you ever need a source for laughter,
look no further than the worries of your past.

What folly to think that every pain leads to worse.
All fear is based on what we perceived to have
happened to others.

To those who search the fogs of tomorrows for
troubles that can be prepared for today, Heaven
thanks you for the laughter.

When you worry, you set into motion the building
of a bridge with no lights that connects you to
events that don't yet exist. A poor use of energy.

The drama that we support around a problem often
uses the vital energy that is needed for the solution.

Often, our fears of aging do more harm
than aging ever would.

It is usually not the lack of hard work but the
intense worrying about a poor outcome that
practically guarantees the poor outcome.

The universal remedy is not some rare flower or expensive drug but the simple virtue of patience. With patience, all will change.

Change will always be your constant companion throughout your life. If you embrace change, fear will remain small and amusing.

Many situations have the ability to influence what happens to you but whether your heart smiles or frowns is still your conscious choice.

The problems that you have right now can be solved with what you have right now if you are willing to compromise.

To sit in a tropical paradise and think thoughts of freezing weather seems absurd until you close your eyes to the beauty around you and worry.

If you could follow the advice that you would give to someone else with the same problem, all of your problems would be short-lived.

Anxiety is only summoned by fear of loss. If your focus is on that part of you that cannot be lost, anxiety soon withers and dies.

We don't know all of the aspects of what is actually happening right now, and yet, we make ourselves very upset because we are sure that we know exactly what might happen.

The first step to change your life is to fire fear and insecurity, for they have covered the windows and convinced you of the darkness. The second step is to uncover the windows.

Sometimes the darkness is just God taking you through a tunnel so you won't have to climb over the whole mountain.

In order for depression to dominate the mood of a person, a person must believe the two lies that happiness is to be found outside of oneself and only by the very fortunate.

As we approach some of the doorways in our life, fear of change is guarding them. Those who turn back will never know that more courage is given with each step forward.

Hold up a penny and ask yourself which side is more powerful, the heads or the tails. Not only are they absolutely equal, but they both are intrinsic parts of the whole. The feminine and the masculine are equal parts of existence. To know one is not to know the other. You could know everything about the heads side of a coin and still be totally ignorant of the other side. What we need to learn is the sanctity and complete power of both. If we want to work on lessening our anger or hostility, it won't work to keep thinking about anger and hostility. You must incorporate the opposites. You start thinking about love and compassion, and anger and hostility start to automatically shrink.

What is the opposite of what you are struggling with?

It is the problem that we can find no answer to that diminishes our ego, causes us to seek, and pulls us out of our comfort zone. In other words, it is one of our greatest gifts.

One of the paradoxes in life is that the more security that you give up by going on adventures, the greater your ability to feel secure.

The "what if" key opens the doors of both dreams and fears. Try the door that appears less used.

We are constantly on alert for anything that could possibly go wrong with our health, our finances, our relationships, or our home and eventually we become blind to all that is going right.

It is impossible to erase the old tapes that constantly play in your mind. You can, however, continually record over them with positive thoughts that will play instead.

The very first step in finding peace of mind and clarity is to consciously rise above the pettiness that swirls around you.

Thoughts that are dark and seemingly contrary to who we believe we are will appear. Cast them aside immediately, or study them and get caught in the quicksand of doubt.

Oh, how we devour every morsel of a catastrophe even when we are not personally affected. Is it any wonder that we create a banquet from our own problems?

Worry is like having a twenty foot ladder in a one story house in case something happens. It is never of any use and too much of your time is involved with wondering what to do with it.

You label parts of your life correctly when you compare them to fertilizer, but you stop there instead of celebrating the flowers that will blossom from it. More fertilizer, more flowers. Bring it on!

We would never be ashamed to have too big a diamond or too many hundred dollar bills, but put on a couple of pounds and we're suddenly ashamed.

We see our mistakes as a sign of our weakness and imperfection. Do we find fault with the babies who falter in their steps or do we cheer them on?

What happened to all the dire straits that you fearfully sailed through? Just like the next one, they go right by no matter how much or little you worry.

When a crisis touches you tangentially or even further away than that, your ego still wants to make it personal. A deep breath and an awareness of the truth will set you free.

Every time that we climb over an obstacle, we get a different perspective than we had. Sometimes good luck is the only reason for the obstacle.

A small crack in the sidewalk does not impede our travel, so why then does a small break in the flow of money make us believe that the path to our dreams is closed?

Nothing narrows your happiness faster than doubt.
Nothing drains it of energy faster than worry.

The most exercise most imaginations get is when
they are used to describe how bad things are.

Carefully you reach through the thorns to
experience the joy of the berry. When sad,
reach through the thorns of your life and
pick something to enjoy.

Make a list of everything that bothers you.
Look at it one year from now and after you stop
laughing, change.

If we are not constantly thinking about the good times, thinking about the blessings, thinking about God's love for us, thinking about the wonderful people we have known, thinking about who we love, we are most likely going to be thinking about things that do not bring us joy. Something is going to grow in our garden. If we do not plant what we want to grow, it makes no sense to be upset at what we get to harvest. How close are you to joy? As close as your next thought.

What are you thinking about?

Peace and tranquility are yours for the taking.
All you have to do is limit the amount of
things you let upset you.

If we were to be totally free of problems for
one hour, we would not enjoy it because we
would spend that hour searching for where
the problems were hiding.

A house where nothing is thrown away would soon
be taken over by garbage. Learn to throw away
those thoughts that clutter up your life.

Everything will always change and not all of the
changes will be to your liking. Seek peace of
mind as a refuge and as a way of life.

Never wish away today's crisis, for it is giving you the tools and strength to easily handle another.

Problems are like movie theaters. When you walk into one from being in the light, it can seem much darker than it really is, but a little pause, and you realize that there is light there too.

If you watch a storm upon the ocean you would think that all was turbulent, but if you could see under the surface, you would see the calm. Learn to touch that place within yourself that is always calm.

Yesterday's troubles are like yesterday's news, not that interesting and not that relevant.

Nature has no fury to equal the storm that
we can create in our own minds.

You would think someone crazy if you saw them
yelling and crying and begging the ocean at low tide
for the tide to rise again. Yet, we do that with the
low tides in our lives.

Nothing will prevent difficult days from appearing in
your life. Nothing is to be gained by making other
days difficult by worrying about when those days
will appear.

Worry and its companion, complaining, are the
twins that illegally park themselves in front of your
heart when it is closed.

For as much as you fret and worry, all of your needs in every second of your life have been taken care of quite nicely.

There will always be a negative alternative to any positive thought. Its mere appearance should never be seen as proof of a negative outcome.

It's not in wanting more that we become anxious. It is forgetting to take into account what we already have.

If you yell and flail at an ocean wave, you will be knocked over. If you duck and let it go past harmlessly, you will always keep your balance.

If you believe that someday in the future you will
laugh at what you are going through, why wait?

Worry requires a strong belief system.
You must believe that tomorrow contains
a poison that you can sample today.

Dramas are the dark bridges that link our troubles.
Without those bridges, we would have to walk
through valley after valley of joy.

Disturbing thoughts can come from many
sources, but their strength and longevity is
solely dependent upon your attention.

When you are falling, it's a bad time to ask not to be falling, but it's an excellent time to ask for a soft landing.

No matter how difficult everything may seem at times, you are never further away from the path than one conscious breath.

You are the luckiest person in the world because every time that you thought things were working out for the worst, they were really working out for the best.

The captain of a ship does not waste time asking the storm why. He focuses all of his awareness on getting through it.

We would never hold on to a problem past its point
of solution unless it was dressed up in the juiciness
of drama. Very few problems are naked.

Hold a difficult day as you would a sick child,
and the day and you will heal.

Fear comes into our life riding on the unknown.
It is our obsession with control, to know the
answer to everything that is happening to us,
that gives him his trusty steed.

The tragedy is not that problems befall us;
the tragedy is that we become more attached
to the drama of the problem than to the
search for a solution.

We constantly inflate our fears with worry
and then we justify our worrying by pointing
out the size of our fears.

Worry has never solved or derailed
an approaching problem.

Only with an undisciplined mind are we capable
of inflicting wounds on ourselves from something
that will never happen.

Of all the things that we worry about, so few will
actually happen. And of those, very few actually
have the capacity to change our lives in any
meaningful way.

Each life has its share of suffering and there is no magic elixir to keep it away. Each time it appears, in whatever form, help someone who suffers more.

Sometimes, the only way to get to a higher level is to wade through a bit of madness. The madness doesn't impede your journey, but the fear of it might.

'Tis the wailing and the yelling that keeps us transfixed on the drama when the wailing should be for the time wasted.

Worrying brings forth a thousand frightening scenarios that can disturb our minds and upset our bodies, and yet, have no possibility of ever happening.

Wishing will not get rid of a great fear. Only a greater fear or a greater passion can replace it.

Everything that you run towards gets larger. The only exception is fear. As you run towards it, it gets smaller and smaller.

The strength that you can summon to deal with problems is greatly influenced by whether you approach those problems as a drama or an adventure.

Disenchantment does not suddenly drop into a person's life. It is home-grown out of a failure to accept that you are not the controller of everything and everybody.

No one relaxes in a control tower because it is a place of high alert and anxiety. To relax, one must come down a few levels. Get out of your thoughts and into your heart.

One of the greatest mood enhancers is putting on some good music and dancing alone.

When we feel off balance and unable to think clearly, we usually search for answers in that darkness. It is better to search for the light first.

We make our workplace safe so that no one will be hurt, but we ignore the worry that will take more souls than the most dangerous job.

You cannot expect to get out of a place where you are stuck without a big expenditure of energy. Simply complaining more will never accomplish it.

When you worry you weaken the only part of you that could come up with the solution.

The possibility that you may be able to change what is going on in your life is directly related to how involved you are with the drama of it all.

Courage is not the absence of fear. It is the refusal to feed fear when it does show up.

The most useless thing to possess is worry.
A suitcase full of most things has value,
but a warehouse full of worry won't even
buy a small button.

Faith

When you love someone so much that they are all
that you can think about, you'll know exactly how
Heaven feels about you.

Therapy can help you find the source of your
problems but spirituality can help you find the
source of your strength.

Compared to the size of the seed, the amount of
dirt that a sprout has to push through to reach the
light is enormous. The same power that helps every
seed is always helping you.

Overwhelmed with too many things that
have to be done in too short a time, we stop
for a moment to wonder what does it all mean
and Heaven shouts "AHA!"

A hand held right in front of your eyes blocks you
from seeing anything but held at arms length,
everything else is visible. Don't let your problems
obscure the view of your blessings.

O, those poor loving souls that heroically
bear torment so that compassion may
awaken in the rest of us.

A tear is shed in heaven every time that
we exclaim that no one loves us.

Like fine crystal, a life may be perfect one moment
and shattered the next, but unlike shattered crystal,
the Maker of the life can put it back together.

Saying that you have no time for spirituality is like saying that you have no time for breathing. Both are part of everything you do.

When despair or fear seems to overwhelm you and what is left of your sanity cries out for relief, send your love to heaven and a lifeline will appear.

If you read about the ultra rich, you feel lacking. If you read about the ultra poor, you feel guilty. If you read about God, you feel perfect. Choose wisely.

We know that contemplating our problems repeatedly can make us feel miserable. Surprise! Repeatedly contemplating our blessings can make us feel good.

Boredom is wanting change but not getting it and anxiety is wanting stability but getting change. Heaven gladly accepts the surrender of either.

If you were going on a week's vacation, you could think of nothing else, and yet, knowing that you are going to heaven, you rarely give it thought.

Our love of an artist depends on whether or not we love what he creates. How can we love God if we hold in contempt anything that god has created?

If you identify with your body, sickness will color your thoughts and spoken words, but if you identify with your spirit, sickness changes nothing.

Willingness to change and faith are the golden keys
that unlock the door to opportunity.

To be in a play and to pay no attention to the
Director would make an actor feel lost and out of
sync with what was going on.

Faith gives us the ability to have something turn out
totally different from what we had planned and
believe that it is a better way.

If you don't practice finding your connection to
Heaven when it is light, how will you ever find it
when you need it in the dark?

When you are fearful, you can't talk yourself
out of it because the voice that talks is the voice
that is scared. Go beyond words and breathe
in the peace of Heaven.

Sometimes, our path seems to have disappeared.
These are the times when we must climb to a higher
level to find where it continues.

Never believe that mere knowledge of God's
existence will in any way take the place of loving
and yearning for God.

Faith is a matter of looking at this moment and
believing that no matter what is going on - it is the
very best thing that could be happening.

We believe that if we could find a clear connection to God we would be very grateful, not realizing that being very grateful is the clear connection to God.

One of the first steps to embracing gratitude is to stop complaining and to start thanking God for your current level of health. It could be a lot worse.

An extensive knowledge of words can give us the ability to accurately describe everything in existence with two exceptions: God and love.

Each one of us goes in directions that seem contrary to our plans but Heaven knows that it is the only way for others to cross our path.

It is only in professing our love to Heaven that we learn how to profess our love honestly on earth.

Silence is not a vacuum seeking to be filled. It is a delicate place where you can discern the difference between idle chatter and the whispers of God.

We move through life like a wave upon the ocean encountering winds and currents that change our direction and force but never our oneness with the ocean.

A definition of the Divine is the most useless. An acceptance of the Divine is the most priceless.

Look to people for advice. Look to nature for examples. Look to Heaven for perfection.

Doing the right thing while thinking otherwise gains no merit.

Read history books to see how there have always been problems. Read sacred books to see how to always handle them.

Soon, age will make meaningless all that you held as youthful, but your soul will not be even one moment older than when you were born.

Don't pity the person that has a different belief than you. Pity the person who has none.

A prayer is the spark and your faith is the fire that lights and warms even the coldest and darkest nights.

If you ever see an angel, the first thing that you'll notice is that their wings are bigger than they need to be. It is for when we throw ourselves into despair and they gently lift us out.

Seriousness perpetuates itself by fooling you into believing that you can dig yourself out of a hole. Lightness reminds you to stop digging and climb out.

If there was a special pair of glasses that allowed
you to see all of the help and love that is always
surrounding you, there would be no need for faith
unless you lost the glasses.

Oh, the golden day when you decide once and for
all to stop juggling all those balls, only to find out
that they continue to be juggled perfectly by
Heaven.

One of the real dangers on the spiritual
path is creating a crisis or serious problem so
that you can test how powerful you have grown.
That's ego, not spirit.

There are doors in our life that we throw ourselves
against and still they refuse to open, but when we
surrender and shed our tears, it is those very tears
that open the door.

Many people are humbled before they are
given great power. Heaven knows that if a person
can't handle humility, they will never be able
to handle power.

Remember when you were very young and you felt
such a strong connection to God and nature? That is
your real, ever present, inner child.

The biggest delusion on your spiritual path is
believing that you are conscious and very few
others are. It's just more us and them stuff that
takes you back to the starting point.

A song is Heaven's gift to use when your mind is
filled with too many thoughts or with thoughts that
don't feel so good.

If you turn your back on God, nothing bad will happen, but there will be this feeling that you have lost something precious.

Worry leads to fear and fear leads to panic. Faith leads to love and love leads to strength. The path of worry demands a blindfold and the path of faith demands that you take it off.

Instead of just randomly worrying about everything, find one thing that God has no hand in and worry about that.

What force propels a person forward when they don't have the strength for another step? It is the force of all of the people who pray for them whether known to them or not.

Spiritual blindness is the affliction of believing that God is gone from your sight. If we believe that God is everything and that God is love, then obviously everything has not gone from sight and love is still around. So God must still be around.

Do you think that it may be our failure to perceive an ever-present God that is the problem?

A parent could never be disappointed because a child fell down while learning to walk because it is expected. God could never be disappointed in you for anything either.

When you say that you can't handle one more problem, you are throwing down the gauntlet to heaven. Heaven will send you more problems just to prove to you how strong you really are.

When a serious problem arises, we pause our spiritual quest in order to give the problem our full attention not realizing that the problem was an answer to how to be more spiritual.

In case you were wondering: your calling is to love, heal, and serve.

Gardening is not just a one day affair for weeds would soon overtake the beauty you planted. If we wish to have a loving nature, it will take more than one day of church or temple.

Faith plus effort is better than a tremendous amount of effort alone.

In reality we are not always good, that is something learned, but we are always holy because we come from God.

Most of us would be full of fear in the Amazon jungle alone, but an experienced guide would alleviate those fears. Remember that you always have an experienced Guide as you go through this life.

Everything around you is influenced by how you act,
and how you act is influenced by what you think,
and what you think is influenced by how well you
feed your soul.

If all we see is dark shadows In front of us,
there is nothing to fear for that means that
the light is right behind us.

A fish swims the seven seas looking for this special
thing called water. A seeker walks the streets and
trails looking for this special thing called God.

Everything in life is possible with one exception.
And that exception is that no one can walk alone.

You are going to make it through whatever is troubling you, but without your prayers it's going to be a little slower.

Hold fast to your dreams. Only time will tell if they are yours to enjoy or if Heaven knew that you would keep them alive for someone else.

When traveling someplace unknown,
we quickly become anxious if there are no signs.
On the road of life, Heaven loves you so much that
there are always signs.

The child is unaware of their needs being taken care of and the adult is unaware of how many of their prayers have been answered.

We search in vain for a way out of the darkness but if we just find the light, the way out will become apparent.

You can't make a leap of faith from lying on the couch. You have to be up and running in order to make a good leap.

When someone prays for peace in the world, they are praying for you because without your peace, the world can't have it.

It is the seriousness of our search for answers that takes us away from the laughter that could enlighten us.

Only after hitting the bottom do you realize that you weren't dashed to pieces by the fall, and then it becomes very obvious that Someone caught you.

You were deemed able to hear the message because you were deemed capable of spreading the message.

We work and pray to attain a goal and once we have it, we forget that work and prayer are necessary in order to keep it.

Problems are much easier to solve if God is in the equation.

How much you want to punish the evil doers
in this world is equal to how harshly you judge
yourself. That's why the masters teach you to love
your enemies.

There are those times when you just feel out of
balance. This is the worst time to put your faith on
hold while you search for answers.

To appreciate the flower on the plant takes an eye
for beauty. To appreciate the flower in the seed
takes a soul with faith.

How we long for the ability to be as witty as others
and yet, the words of the wise pass us by unnoticed.

Knowledge of the latest news is not the way to find importance in your life. The one and only reason for the news is to tell you where to direct your prayers.

Your purpose in life will never be known until you reflect back on your entire life and the end of your days. If you knew sooner, there would be no need for faith.

Thinking is what makes the mind confused. More thinking about how to unconfuse the mind is pointless. Don't think, pray.

No matter how fast and far you are running into negativity, it can be stopped and reversed the second that you consider the light.

A spiritual practice encompasses many things. We read, pray, meditate, and think that we are done. But that was only the easy work. The hard work is pulling ourselves away from anger and resentment and negativity. The hard work is holding our tongue and not spreading gossip about those we dislike. The hard work is forgiveness and going out of our comfort zone to help someone else.

Are you strong enough for some hard work?

No one gets to drive while the fight over the keys goes on. No one gets to enlightenment while the fight over words goes on.

When we are physically hungry, we go to the food, but foolishly, when we are spiritually hungry, we wait for a delivery.

Some decisions will work out fine and some not so fine. If you believe that Heaven helped you on one and abandoned you on the other, you're wrong.

Security will always be a few dollars away, but serenity will always be as close as a few prayers.

Some days you need a shield and some days you need a sword. Every day you need heavenly guidance on which one to use.

We practice diligently to master a sport or a language or an instrument but believe that a spiritual life is just something that happens to people.

A child that falls and scrapes a knee is not any less loved or protected. No matter what happens in your life, you are loved and protected.

Fear is merely the warning light that goes on when you are low in faith.

If you wish to pray effectively, you must pray from who you really are and not from the mask you wear.

The anguish that comes from trying to find a reason for something terrible that happened can only be relieved by surrendering to the infallibility of Thy will.

Sometimes when we look for hope and see nothing, we despair and forget that hope is invisible. It is only when we sprinkle faith in front of us that we can clearly see it.

You don't have to force yourself to believe in a higher power. Just think about all of the times you were pulled back from the brink and it's pretty obvious.

There are always difficult choices to be made.
When choosing, always take into account the fact
that you have always, without exception, found the
strength you needed.

Feeling good solely because someone else is feeling
good is a joy that can never be known by those who
are consumed by how they themselves are feeling.

When spirituality is only a one day affair, then six-
sevenths of life will be a burden.

When you want something very badly and it doesn't
happen, it is the love of Heaven that overlooks your
"please" so that something better can happen.

Whether you have problems or not is not a reflection of your spiritual growth, but how you handle having some or none speaks volumes.

When you do something charitable but anonymously, you join an elite club whose members are just you and God.

Wanting to connect with God brings you to the gates of heaven but only a fervent yearning to love God can bring you through the gates.

If an expert in medicine can stop you from worrying about sickness then the creator of the universe should be able to stop you from worrying about everything.

Little can be gained and nothing can be changed by looking backward. More problems are solved by looking up rather than by looking back.

Heaven would not provide a bathing suit for you if you were not going swimming. Why would Heaven send you courage if you are not attempting anything?

Sitting beside a bubbling fresh spring it would be absurd to cry about our thirst so how can we cry about a lack of love when Heaven is so close to us?

If your prayers intentionally exclude anyone, that is the hole where the power of our prayers to manifest leaks out.

The amount of pain that you feel after a disappointment is no reflection of your spiritual progress but how long you hold on to the pain is a pretty good indicator.

We dedicate books and buildings and songs but to whom do we dedicate our daily work? The answer to that question determines our stress level more than anything else.

It is our thoughts that spawn our troubles and it is our prayers that bail us out.

Discussing religion, no matter how in depth the discussion, should never be confused with actually practicing that religion.

You'll not be judged on the correctness of your beliefs, but on whether you used your beliefs as wings or whips.

Faith isn't a connection to Heaven or to each other. Faith is the light that allows you to see that the connection already exists.

Serenity is the realization that you don't know all the answers but Heaven does.

Disappointment only lingers when we cling to the idea that the way we wanted things to work out was better than the way God has planned.

There are two times in life when a person's face
turns toward Heaven. The first is in great prayers
and the second is in great laughter.

Prayer is the only antidote for a mind that is
poisoned by unwanted thoughts.

The first step to reclaiming your happiness is to fire
your ego and to reinstate your spirit as the guiding
force in your life.

If the hardest rock will eventually yield to a constant
flow of water, then the obstacles in your life will
eventually yield to constant prayer.

The only thing more beautiful than a flower in bloom is the essence within that flower that gave birth to the bloom.

Heaven has given us the strength to stand tall through any mistake but it is the replaying of that mistake that brings us to our knees. It is not Heaven's finger on the replay button.

Sometimes the most difficult people in our lives are the people closest to us. Heaven didn't want us to have to waste time traveling to our teachers.

All great things will eventually flow towards you and the time now spent on questioning your luck would be better spent on patience and faith.

If you gave someone more than enough food, and water, and clothes, and shelter, and they said only a quick thanks to you now and then, you would know why Heaven sighs.

Faith is the immunizing factor that tells you that if fear show up, even if it's all around you, you're protected.

A sick body on a solid spirit is like tattered sails on a fine ship. It won't go fast, but it will never sink.

Being serious and humorless in our search for enlightenment is only a quest for something serious and humorless.

Meditation gives you the tools to
clean the window; simply looking through the
cleaned window is called insight.

You are not the one that is causing your heart to
beat while you wake and sleep. Every second, your
heartbeat is an affirmation of Heaven.

Tangible or intangible, consider losing that which is
most dear to you and you will have the barest hint
of how Heaven feels about you.

Boredom is the ability to close one's eyes to God,
Love, and Gratitude and convince oneself that there
is nothing to do. A remarkable feat considering
what surrounds us.

The true test of compassion is how you react when
something bad happens to someone you dislike.

How often does the something wrong
warning go off in your mind? If you believe that
you are in charge, quite often; but if you know
that Heaven is in charge, rarely.

A ship going around a dangerous storm
will take longer to reach its destination.
Why do we question Heaven when our dreams do
not materialize on our timetable?

Faith is a sturdy ship in a sea of troubles and hope is
the life preserver thrown by Heaven whenever we
fall overboard.

Looking for your purpose in life is like poking around
with a sword looking for something that is sharp
and has a point.

Living in the light doesn't mean that you
won't have any stupid periods. It just
guarantees that they will be well lit.

The finest clay in the hands of the greatest artists
can only become a well sculpted piece of clay. But
should that artist subject the clay to a great fire, a
masterpiece is born.

Never let an interpretation of enlightenment
masquerade as true enlightenment.
Enlightenment is an experience and not an
accumulation of knowledge.

Sometimes we act like the little child in the car seat with a little plastic steering wheel in front of him. He looks through the windshield and turns the plastic wheel from side to side, convinced that he is driving the car. The person driving the car allows this act to go on, smiling at the fierce concentration of the little one. Isn't this how we live our life? Aren't we convinced that we are solely responsible for the twists and turns in our life? We need to give credit to who is really doing the driving. We need to have faith that we are going by the best route for everyone involved.

Are you making believe that you are in charge?

Worry stems from the recurring thought that you
are unprepared for something, real or imagined. If
you have an abundance of love and faith, you are
prepared for anything.

The troubles that you are having are not
driving you into the arms of God. Like a fussy child,
you are having your troubles in the arms of God.
You never left.

The moment you were given life you
were given love. The length of living is in
Someone else's hands but you are being trusted
with the amount of loving.

If you are not holding the hand of God while you
live each moment, you are going to have to leap for
it when you die and that is the basis for all fear.

What hides in the shadows of future days
no one really knows, but a bearer of light
has no fear of shadows.

A philosophy that is just accepted and not forged in
the fires of errors and tempered in midnight's tears
will fall apart the moment it is tested.

We smile at a child who is being very serious over
an insignificant problem because we know that our
problems are the serious ones and then God smiles.

God gave us the gift of boredom
so that we couldn't find a small,
safe place and spend all of our time there.

Your path is Divinely built and you
can walk nowhere else. Now whether you
constantly bounce off the guardrails or walk in
peace, that part is up to you.

We have no doubt whatsoever that Heaven guides
everyone in the world and yet we simultaneously
harbor doubt that Heaven is guiding our children.

No matter what befalls us, we will adapt and move
on. We may give the credit to courage but it is
always a courage born of grace.

Our mind is always seeking happiness and will settle
for a temporary fix, but our soul is always seeking
the source of happiness and nothing else will do.

The pain that we endure from a surgeon fixing us is understandable. Allow the pain that we endure from Heaven fixing us to be understandable too.

The concept of mind over matter is fragile because mind can fail. Spirit over mind and matter on the other hand never fails.

The difference between the whispers of your mind and the whispers of Heaven is that the whispers of Heaven will guide and inform you but never criticize you.

If we find it easier to worry than to have faith it is only because we have been practicing one more than the other.

Sometimes when we flirt with madness, we
completely forget that we are married to Heaven.

Say good morning to the day,
dismiss your judgment, smile at everyone
you meet, be grateful for your food and health
and you can skip your prayers.

A burst of anger, saying something unkind, is a facet
of your humanness. As an apology, feeling bad for
hurting another is a facet of your divinity.

Sometimes we miss the blessings that are coming
our way because we were stooping down to find
some criticism to throw.

When you reach out to help someone else, Heaven holds all of your worries so that they don't get in your way.

We find no time to celebrate life because we are standing ever vigilant to the earliest signs of something going wrong in our life. Nothing but faith can relieve us from that post.

When what you are wanting is not what you are getting, have faith that what you are getting is what you need. Reflection and not resistance is the key to understanding.

Surrendering to a higher power is simply saying that you will acknowledge who is really driving. It doesn't change the ride but it does free you up to help the other passengers.

Most of us are stuck at the level of duality. We choose which shoe, the right or the left, is the best and then we spend our lives defending that shoe and denigrating the other shoe and all who have chosen it. That battle will wage until we can see that they are essentially the same. A Master is one who sees shoes, and not right or left.

What do you see?

Just because a parent is in the playground with a child doesn't mean that the child can't fall and scrape a knee. Heaven will heal and console you but it won't keep you in a bubble.

Financial problems coupled with health problems, which they often are, are one of the most difficult paths out there. Heaven has to deem you very competent to allow you to try it.

Because we have practiced, we tie our shoes quickly when they become untied. How quickly we deal with our mind when it unravels depends upon our spiritual practice.

In the same way that we put away a
favorite warm coat in the summer,
Heaven puts away some favorite things
of ours because we won't be needing them.

Seeing yourself in another person, compassion is yours. Seeing God in another person, devotion is yours. Seeing God in yourself, Heaven is yours.

Making a decision when both possibilities seem equal can be difficult unless you remember that Heaven ensures that any choice you make is exactly what you need.

Something shared with a loved one is greater by far than something experienced alone. But a life shared with Heaven tops them all.

Never see yourself as losing value for any reason whatsoever. No matter how worn a hundred dollar bill gets, it will never be worth less because we have faith in who made it.

Taking care of our work and family, we often become frustrated that there is no time left for our spiritual practice until we are reminded that those too are our spiritual practice.

All of the answers that we seek are available if we would just look up, but we walk with our gaze downward until we trip and fall and finally the only way we can look is up.

Over there beyond the highway flares is a scene that will be remembered in your prayers or in your gossip. Which would you rather have if it were you?

A mistake is God's way of saying: "Pay attention!"

Once you truly and consistently see yourself as a child of God, material possessions can no longer lure you with a promise of having an identity.

A prayer by itself is just a beautiful poem. It is the loving repetition of a prayer that turns in it into a generator of miracles.

It is not that one religion is right and all of the others are wrong. All are trying as best as they can to describe a love that is beyond words.

It is foolish to inject water into every single leaf on a tree when we can just water the roots. Feed your soul and every area of your life will be nourished.

When faced with incompetence,
how far back do you have to stand until you
can see it as part of the Divine plan?

It is unnecessary to spend time in prayer
for what you need. That time is better spent
praying for patience, for what you truly
need is always on its way to you.

It doesn't take a miracle to lift the shade by yourself
and let the light in. However, it will take a miracle to
let the light in if you are just going to sit there.

Holding on to what we think is best for ourselves is
the biggest obstacle to getting what heaven knows
is best for us.

You have the answer to doing something better than it is currently being done. The only thing that holds back its implementation is one drop of courage and two drops of faith.

You get no help when you show Heaven your shackled hands because Heaven knows that you still have the key that was given to you.

Anxiety screams that we must do something. Prayer happily yells back that we have found something to do.

You don't help someone trapped in a well by jumping in and talking to them. You find something that connects you both and then you pull from a higher place.

I always walk our dog, Jackie, down the same street when leaving our house. One morning I saw broken glass up ahead where a bottle had been broken. I pulled Jackie to go in a different direction, and she put up a terrific struggle. She wanted to keep going the way she had always gone and refused to turn. She pulled so hard against her collar that she started to cough. No matter what I said, or how I said it, she wanted to keep going the same way. There was no way that I was going to let her get hurt, so I forced her to go a different way. She was upset for quite a while, but I knew that she was better off. I thought about how often I rebel against a change of direction in my life.

How often do we curse the detour instead of celebrating the blessed guidance?

Most people reflect more on their weight than on their spirit, and yet, in a hundred years, both will weigh nothing but one will still be alive.

The person who masters sacred words can teach endlessly, but the person who has mastered sacred intent need only to live, and by living, teach.

If your prayers do not seem to be answered, maybe it is because you are in an area of poor reception. Try moving closer to Heaven.

Pay no attention to the fears that swirl around your troubles for there is nothing that can happen to you that you do not have the spiritual tools to handle.

The same force that takes care of us
while we sleep, ready to awaken us should
the need arise, is sadly left on the pillow as
our ego resumes command upon waking.

God is the difference
between alone and lonely.

Sometimes our steps are slow and difficult only
because we carry all of those whom we have not
forgiven.

When you don't feel Heaven's support for which
choice to make, it may be because Heaven's
support is behind choosing neither.

Having found a path to Heaven, progress remains elusive to some because they belittle the other paths instead of walking the one they found.

What matters if darkness is everywhere but where you step?

Each morning you have many choices but the one that will affect you the most is choosing whether you or a higher power is going to be in charge today.

Just when you think that your dreams are out of reach, Heaven can show you a shortcut.

Through religious training or meditation, many have been given the cloak of serenity but so few wear it.

Faith is the fast acting glue at the end of your rope.

When everything is changing, pray for courage. When nothing is changing, pray for patience. When you don't know, pray for clarity, courage, and patience.

If you think that someone is not being cared for because you can't be there, then who do you think takes care of the seas and the forests when you are not there?

There are so many times during the day when you are fully capable of talking with God and if you consciously look and listen, you will know that you are being heard. As your feet hit the floor in the morning, let God be your first thought. As you pick up your feet to climb into bed at night, let God be your last thought. When I am driving by myself talking to God and I don't feel connected, I turn off the radio and ask God to give me a sign when I turn it back on. I think about God exclusively for several minutes. And when I get the feeling to turn it back on, 9 times out of 10, there is a word or phrase in the song that lets me know without a doubt that God is listening. Of course sometimes my expectancy is met with a hemorrhoid commercial or some such. But, thankfully, it's rare. Most of the time, I am brought nearly to tears by what I hear.

What do you do to connect?

The basis for our upsets is that
our plans were superseded by those of Heaven.
We think that the problem is our plans,
but the problem is really our pride.

The person who searches for the light is
usually unaware that it is with a light that is being
ignored that they are searching.

In a self-centered life, failure gives birth to the
regret that we are like other people who fail. In a
soul-centered life, failure gives birth to a
compassion that others who fail feel as we do.

Letting go is not an act of strength for all the
strength in the world will not make it easier.
Letting go is an act of faith.

Our spiritual growth can be measured
by how quickly we give up the friends who
will not support us in our dislikes.

Sacred words are not the truth for the truth is
experienced and not merely read about, but sacred
words are the directions to experience the truth.

When you don't know what to do,
pray, but remember that you are not praying
for the answer, it's already here. You are praying
for the clarity to see it.

If you are one hundred percent,
absolutely sure that God is in your life,
then life is all about opening your presents.

Nothing is more confusing than trying to be yourself
if you don't know who you are. Embrace the Divine
and the masks will drop off one by one.

Age can slow the body and disease can fog the
mind. If a well worn path to the soul has not been
trod, where will serenity be found?

We rarely change voluntarily. That is why Heaven
must sometimes manipulate our supply of money to
get us to where we need to be.

A person who truly dedicates their life to
God has no need to seek a purpose in life.

You would not willingly let fear into your life;
that is why it always comes disguised as concern.
Only faith can expose the charlatan
and render him powerless.

You don't have to pray forever.
You just have to pray until your first
response to every situation is love.

We say a child is grown up when they
can play outside and be confident enough
to know that a loving protector is close by without
actually having to see them.

When you don't return Heaven's calls,
it puts a sacred book, a rainbow,
or a friend right in front of you.

Even before your prayer is answered, praying has given you the gift of humility. Humility is the key to the first lock that opens the door to miracles.

Clarity is not the ability to hear whispered directions. It is the discernment of whether the whispers are from your ego or your soul.

The urge to lie will always equal the fear of telling the truth. The deciding factor will be the strength of your spirit.

Making a mistake shows that Heaven has absolute confidence that you are strong enough for another lesson.

Freedom is not the ability to do whatever you want. It is the ability to choose from everything available what is best for your soul.

Faith gives us the ability to look at our lives and, seeing no great supply of courage, believe that it will appear whenever we need it.

It is hard to see a pattern in a handful of wool but in the hands of a master weaver, the pattern soon appears. Some people may appear as a handful of wool, but remember whose hands they are in.

Listen closely to the whispers of Heaven so that you can find guidance to walk past the irritations in order to get to the inspirations.

If we truly embraced our own beliefs,
we would not find fault with the beliefs
of anyone else.

To believe that you made a bad decision
you must also believe that Heaven blinked.

The giving of an anonymous gift is the best
way to starve your ego and feed your soul.

Never let the excitement of the news substitute
for the excitement of all of the love and
all of the blessings in your life.

Faith and worry cannot coexist for long. As one gets stronger, the other gets weaker. Faith's home is our spirit and worry's home is in our body. All of the great masters have exhorted us for millennia to give much more attention to our spirit rather than our body, and yet, somehow, we still believe that if lost or gained enough weight, grew or shrunk a few inches, lost or gained a few years, grew or lost some hair, fixed our eyes, teeth, nose, butt, muscles, posture, we would have everlasting happiness. Even if we did all those things, we couldn't be completely happy because we would worry that it would someday be gone... and it will!

Are you preoccupied with the physical or the spiritual?

If a person needs to be tested, Heaven gives them problems. If a person needs to be severely tested, Heaven gives them luxury.

If there is any part of your life that you are unwilling to lay in the lap of God, then you must believe that there is something in existence that is yours and not God's.

You can be surrounded by dozens of loving people or absolutely none, but it will not matter at all if you have fallen in love with God.

It is in the quiet time, with no one else around, that we truly understand that we are never alone.

When we can't help someone whom we love, we worry. By worrying, we block ourselves from feeling any joy and darken the world for us and them. Pray and light two lives.

So many people drown in desperation while waiting for a sign that all is well, forgetting that it is only in loving and trusting God that all things become well.

Some changes we can see coming. Fear them and you will begin to suffer before they even reach you, but have the faith to love them as Divinely sent and you will trade fear for joyous expectancy.

A constant state of forgiveness
is the lightest way to travel.

We surround ourselves with exercise
equipment to test our strength and
grow stronger. Sometimes, Heaven surrounds us
with problems for the same reason.

Spiritual books are not there to be memorized. They
are there because they have a miraculous ability to
turn on your inner light when you read them.

Being loving is the first step in a being
a student of Heaven. Being loving under
any and all circumstances is the first step
in being a teacher of Heaven.

Heaven never showers a person with opportunity if
the courage to do something with it is lacking.

If you cannot take a step in the direction that
you wish to go no matter how hard you try,
it is obviously the will of Heaven that you
go in a different direction.

Heaven can lift mountains and worlds, but it cannot
lift your head to look in its direction. Only the heart
of one who loves greatly can do that.

Angels don't drive for you, but they always
get out and push when you get stuck.

If we would give half of the thought that we give to
lunch to what good deed we could do today, our
soul would be as well fed as our bodies.

Wanting things to be different than they are is the prerequisite for any change. But wanting and holding to a certain outcome can be counter-productive to our happiness. The term "Thy will be done" is all about outcomes. No matter how upset or angry we get at a certain outcome, it changes nothing! What happens is always the result of our effort and God's decision. The vast majority of suffering comes from wanting things to be different than they are. "Thy will be done" is not just a nice phrase. It's a way of thinking, a way of life, a way out of quite a bit of suffering.

Can you be in harmony with any outcome?

God isn't in heaven.
God is heaven.

Wisdom

Sometimes there is a feeling that you
need to make a change. It isn't the past
condemning you, it's the future calling back
to you to make the easy change now.

The only thing worse than having a bad day is
ruining a good day by reflecting back on that bad
day.

Self-discipline is not just the ability to say I will do it.
It is the ability to keep saying I will do it over and
over until it is done.

Sometimes we get so caught up in the affairs of the
world, which we can do nothing about, that we
forget about the despair of friends or family that we
can do something about.

Wither thou goest to an annual ball
or to an everyday work, one should always be
prepared to have the time of one's life or thou
should not leave they dwelling.

You can't cleanse the stream if the source is
polluted. You can't fix what happens in your life
unless your thoughts are clear.

Whether things are going right or things
are going wrong won't be a known
for at least a hundred years.

It is safe to look in on where you keep your
wildness locked up. They won't all escape
but you may want to let one or two out before
they reach their expiration date.

The power of a good luck charm is
due in large part to the acceptance that
your life can be improved.

Prosperity is a feeling of gratitude, celebration,
and confidence. It is not something that happens
at a certain dollar amount.

Desires are the rough diamonds that we mine with
our imagination. Only our heart should decide
whether to cut and polish a specific one.

When we have become unconscious of what we
have, it is the gift of adversity that reawakens us to
our blessings in life.

The weak use humor as a razor but weaker still are those who stand there bleeding and force a small laugh instead of a great protest.

Before you think or speak of the world getting darker, check to see if it is instead that your vision is getting narrower and letting less light in.

Your dreams will continue to circle overhead until you clear a space that is free of fear. Only then can they land and come to your aid.

Even if you have to dig very deep, spend one day each week looking for only the good in everyone with no exceptions. On that day, it will be unnecessary to go to church or temple.

You can never just erase a disturbing thought but you can cover it with so much love and forgiveness that it will be almost unrecognizable.

If you don't like the way you look right now, you are really going to hate the way you look in a hundred years. Work on the inside, accept the outside.

Every life has times of frustration and we cannot dodge them but we can protect the people we care about by not letting our frustration make their life difficult too.

Don't put too much emphasis on the mirror because the mirror will never show you what's truly valuable. The pearl is never found on the outside of the oyster.

Each family produces drama but you must decide
whether the love in your family is your story or a
dysfunctional cartoon is your story. One will open
your heart, the other will close it.

The difference between agitation
and love is patience.

All setbacks are minimal unless you want
to be lazy for awhile, and in that case you
can say it was devastating.

An animal will forfeit its freedom by focusing only
on the bait. A person will forfeit their freedom by
only focusing on security.

When we long for the past, we wish that we could have spent that time with more awareness of all of our blessings. We will look back on today similarly.

When we have been wronged, thoughts of vengeance feel good the same way that the scratching of a mosquito bite feels good, but continued, both can lead to a worse problem.

Don't look for new things to change your life. Some fresh beginnings start not with new things but with doing old things in a new way.

The fire burns you only once, but the memory of that fire can burn you a thousand times.
Let go of past hurts.

Planning is good, but planning that is devoid of action is just a blueprint. Some people spend their whole life making blueprints. They get very, very good at making blueprints, but at the end of their life they just have pieces of paper. The person who builds even a shack has something.

What does the blueprint maker have?

One of the greatest things that we can do to help ourselves today and positively affect our tomorrow is to force ourselves to stop complaining.

It is in trying too hard to make something happen that we sometimes stall its progress. The question that looms large then is can we back off without giving up?

We replay our problems over and over again in our minds in our search for a solution but all that does is make us very, very good at replaying our problems.

Every man made object that exists in this world was at one time a solution to a problem. Problems are the midwives of inspiration.

A plane without fuel never flies and even if it is pushed down the runway, it will crash at the end. A dream without a plan is exactly the same.

Your mind is a video library of every moment of your life with commentary. The projectionist always follows your orders but if you give none, he plays anything that gets your attention.

If you wish to quiet your thoughts of self criticism, you won't get there by more thinking. Do something to help another person and suddenly two people feel good about themselves.

Compassion comes from stepping into the shoes of those less fortunate. Ambition comes from stepping into the shoes of those more fortunate.

Honestly, we really don't care about
other people when we judge them.
We just do it to reinforce who we think we are.

If you got a flat tire in front of a place that fixes
flats, you would consider yourself fortunate instead
of unlucky. It's all perspective.

To a stimulus junkie, a moment of anger is not much
different than a moment of pleasure. The key to
mastering your life lies in consciously choosing your
stimulation.

Those who fear the future are soon
overwhelmed by it. Only by running towards
the future are we able to have the momentum
to jump over its obstacles.

There is power associated with telling someone something that they don't know. If it is to inform, we will prosper. If it is to shock, we will become addicted to telling bad news.

Some days you can start out with gratitude and other days you have to start out with forgiveness before you get to gratitude.

Courage is always just a couple of feet away so that if you want it, you have to stand up on your own two feet and take a step in order to get it.

When you are upset about getting upset, you are telling yourself that it is okay to be upset for the right reason. It always feels like the right reason when you get upset.

The person who wishes with a hammer and nails builds faster than the person who sits and wishes.

The sneakiest way to hold on to the past is by convincing yourself that you are looking for the reason something happened as if by knowing the reason you will suddenly let it go.

Our day often turns out exactly like we thought it would not because we could see the future but because when we thought about what would be, we started creating what would be.

Entertaining thoughts about your past being different than it was is a total waste of time and wasting time like that today does not bode well for a happy tomorrow.

Past problems have a tendency to make believe that
they are current problems just to get attention.
Don't fall for it.

An unpaved stretch of road can lead
some to curse the road and others to
give thanks for their shoes.

When we seek to throw criticism at someone we
must first drop the light that we were holding.

One childish belief we have to overcome is the
mindset that the best time of our life
also has to be the most fun.

I was in an airplane leaving Florida and the plane was taxiing to the runway to take off. I was looking out of the window and what do I see standing by a small body of water, but not fifteen feet away – a bald eagle! Symbol of the country and all that. I kept looking out of the window at the bird until I caught the eye of the guy sitting behind me and he asked, "Did you see that? A bald eagle!" And I said, "Yeah, fantastic!" As the plane got to the take off runway – I was thinking that it was probably the first bald eagle I had ever seen in the outdoors. But something kept nagging at me – a bald eagle – that's great but I didn't have that feeling of magnificence that I expected. As we picked up speed, roared down the runway, and lifted off – it dawned on me! The magnificence of the great bald eagle is in flying and soaring and spreading those wings. And then I thought about how much of our magnificence is not perceived by others because we are not soaring and spreading our wings.

In what area of your life are you standing instead of soaring?

Blindly walking past a beggar to attend a conference on world hunger, most of us are so consumed by the big issues that we ignore where we can help right now.

The courage that sobriety brings comes not from refusing to indulge but from a willingness to step into each day believing that being you is enough for anything you will encounter.

Peacefulness does not disappear. It is always there like an ancient treasure covered by sand. Sometimes it naturally appears after a storm and sometimes you have to dig for it.

How quickly we accept the criticism or judgment of another person without considering whether we would believe anything else they said.

We enjoy a sunset or a rainbow or a starry
night or a sunrise because we are not
looking for imperfections.

There is light in every star, breath in every living
body, fish in every ocean and the possibility of sheer
happiness in every moment of your life.

We would never withhold a piece of bread from a
person who was starving. And yet, we judge so
strictly before we give away a kind word.

If you think that tomorrow will never come,
you'll only be right once in your whole life.
If you think that you'll be blessed with another day,
you'll only by wrong once.

When wisdom confronts stupidity,
it is wisdom that seeks silence to
confirm its presence.

The image that we project is directly related to
whether we are focusing on the number of pounds
or the number of blessings.

Life doesn't change one iota,
but the view does.

The hand that is busy pointing blame
never lessens the amount of work to be done.

No matter how hard you work at it, you will never unearth clarity by digging in the mud.

When little things rule,
we play the fool.

Sometimes, we learn from another's example and sometimes, Heaven uses us as an example for someone else.

One of the keys to success is to find out if anyone, anywhere has made it successfully past the limitations that you think you have.

Everyone is trying to find a set of rules that allows life to consistently make sense to them.

Honesty without compassion is like a knife that is all blade and no handle.

Even if you could leave everything behind and set out for paradise on a sailboat, there would still be things you don't want to do onboard the sailboat.

Most people would give everything they own to relive even the worst of their days when they have run out of their days, because now they know the preciousness of any day.

We fear endings the most but that is only
because we believe that there is such a thing.
Actually, there is only transformation, nothing in
existence can just end and disappear.

The turns and twists on the road of life are not
there to confuse you but to slow you down.

Many paths meander through scary places but the
path is never afraid. Always identify with your path
and not with what it is going through.

Hold fast to your ideals but never
hold them so tightly that you can't trade
them for a higher set.

In order to move faster up the ladder of
success, most people lighten their load by
tossing away their humility, compassion, and
honesty, and then complain about the emptiness of
success when they reach the top.

A grain of sand can be analyzed in many different
ways but none will show the beauty of the beach.
No incident in your life defines your life.

There are now enough sources to bolster any side
to any argument about anything. The heart must
now decide what the mind cannot.

A seed can be held in a thousand hands,
but not until it is held by soil or water will it sprout.
When you hold onto something, you may be
preventing it from growing.

We know that our memory is fallible, but we consider our judgment infallible. Yet, our judgment is always based on what we remember.

If a blind person can be happy, then happiness is not a product of what we see. And if a poor person can be happy, then happiness is not a product of what we have.

When we feel trapped in a job or relationship, the first step is to stop concentrating on the drama and then see if we still feel trapped. Sometimes feeling trapped is just the drama.

If we stop and look around, signs of paradise do abound. If we rush with blinding speed, we quickly pass both dreams and needs.

A fantastic seven course meal dumped into
one pot would be totally unappetizing.
Even though you want everything now,
life is better one course at a time.

If your heart is not in it,
the rest of you shouldn't be either.

To see the dawn and be filled with awe is
normal. To see the dawn and be thinking about
something else is considered normal.

Have one vice so that you may blame
everything on it. It minimized the worry
when you don't feel good.

When we are in an expansion phase, we want to go out, socialize, do things, love and travel. When we are in a contracting phase, we want to read, stay home, think about our lives, be loved, and contemplate. If we expand for too long, we lose sight of serenity. If we contract for too long we think too much and become self-centered.

Which phase dominates your life?

A kindness to a child or to an animal is the easiest way to bandage a wounded heart that is too tender for the touch of an adult.

We cheer the changes in seasons and skies and tides, and yet, we are shocked in disbelief at any change in the circumstances in our lives.

If you feel like a balloon in a den of porcupines, the best thing to do is to deflate your ego and walk away without blowing up and scaring the porcupines.

There is no surprise when we see metal moving towards a magnet, and yet, we are bewildered when we are thinking negatively and problems appear.

The gift of solitude is the treasure of living alone, but the gift usually lies unopened fearing that it contains loneliness.

The only reason that you don't celebrate your bad days as a wonderful confirmation of being alive is because no one else does.

Everyone is looking for a map to riches and happiness, but even the most detailed map is useless if you don't know where you are.

Be kind and you will never have to be defensive.

How strictly we wish the laws were enforced on others, but how completely understandable leniency is for us. Awareness is the birthplace of compassion.

An addiction is a refusal to tolerate unhappiness or pain and yet, every addiction increases both.

If you seek serenity first, you will gain the clarity to see upon which path the solution is available.

The time we spend looking for the why something happened is better spent adapting to what happened.

Ego is that part of you that says you are growing and getting better and everyone else is staying the same of getting worse.

If you can't hear an opposing opinion without getting upset then give last call because the mind is getting ready to close.

The thought gives birth to the feeling, and the feeling gives birth to the words, and whether or not the words are spoken gives birth to wisdom.

Seriousness is a particular kind of sight that allows you to see the plant but not the flowers on it.

The wise learn of someone's problem
and seek to help. The unwise merely
take it as food for gossip.

You can learn from books and tapes
and people, but you can truly teach
only from experience.

If you want to succeed in any area of your life,
the first and most important requirement is
to banish all doubt.

It is so odd that so many of the things we wish
for in life, we do nothing but wish for.

True peace comes not from detaching from the world, but in detaching from our notion that we have been in any way shortchanged by life.

When a great blockage to the flow of love needs to be healed, heaven sends a Master. When a small blockage to the flow of love needs to be healed, heaven sends a pet.

Some people blow up their balloon and then look for people with pins. Some people blow up their balloon and then look for people with balloons.

When you get to the end of your rope you will find a place where you can stand on your own two feet.

Of all the shields in the world,
none will hide a heart that is hurt
more poorly than a cleverness with words.

A very sophisticated verbal attack on the way things
are is often confused with actually doing something.

Meditation allows you to understand that we are all
on a carousel and the ride is very frustrating if you
are trying to make your horse win.

Wisdom is information from experience that is
given to the inexperienced so that they will have
confirmation when they have the experience.

Wisdom does not automatically come with age.
Wisdom comes when you have been paying
attention for a long time.

Criticism, by itself, is the perfect way to make
believe that you are passionate about something
without actually having to do anything constructive.

The sufferings in the world are quickly forgotten
when one is in pain, and yet, it is our own pain that
helps us to understand the suffering in the world.

There is no such thing as a wasted day. There are
days that you resisted from start to finish, but that
was you and not the day.

It is not unusual to see someone hush their children
so they could listen to the TV to find out what is
wrong with the world.

Stupidity is not to be mocked, for it is the quickest
shortcut to finding out what doesn't work and
effectively teaching it to others by example.

Just wishing for a change is like
going into a restaurant and telling the
waiter that you are hungry. Nothing gets
delivered to you until you get specific.

Many paths to riches, both material
and spiritual, only seem to be hidden
because they require the bright light of self
confidence to illuminate the first steps.

Frustration is just a wonderful sign telling you that you need to change something very soon. It was never meant to be a place to live.

If the heart grows as youthfulness fades,
no one will notice even the smallest wrinkle.

The end does not come before the beginning and wisdom does not come before the experience.

Pain has nothing to do with you being a good person. Pain has to do with refining this ore one more time to make it even stronger.

When you want, you must be on the same vibrational level as what you want to receive. If you want a job, be sure that you are working - if not at a paying job then at a volunteer position. If you want to be more uplifting, find uplifting people, movies, and music. If you want to grow, find people that will celebrate your growth. If you want a relationship, surround yourself with people who are just like you and not just people who act like you do.

Who or what is influencing you the most?

Instead of telling everyone that you
won't dance because your shoes hurt,
take them off and dance. Never complain
about something that you can change.

A sure sign of your phenomenal good luck
is that every time you are looking for
something that is wrong, you find it.

No one criticizes the clowns for how they are
dressed or how they act because they are a great
source of amusement. Life is a lot funnier when you
realize that all the clowns are not in the circus.

Waiting for what life will give you is like waiting in
front of the oven. If you put something good in, it
will come out even better. But if you put nothing in,
it's a long, hungry wait.

No one ever got rid of something by wrestling with it. When we give up fighting and just say a sincere good-bye and walk away, we have a much better chance to be done with it.

The reason that it is difficult for us to break a bad habit is because when we decide to give up one pleasure, we make ourselves unhappy and unhappiness craves known pleasures.

As long as a flower blooms and a bird sings, the order of the world has not changed at all. What we perceive as great changes are merely ripples on the surface of the ocean.

The most beautiful rug in the world, if only viewed from the underside, would be deemed worthless. Look at every side of a person before you judge them.

Failure is a word that we use as a whip when we wish to punish ourselves or someone else. In truth, it is nothing more than an experience that didn't turn out as planned.

Just like a kite in the sky, your dreams, although they may seem far away, still respond to your every move as long as you hold onto them.

If you expect certain things from life, you are gambling. If you accept all things from life, you are growing.

Last week's newspaper is boring because we can't use the information to tell inform others of what they don't' know and thereby make ourselves important. It's about ego, not the news.

There is a moment between finding out that someone else was wrong and celebrating that you were right that defines your level of maturity.

Thinking can be a fine way to live and learn, but beware that thinking doesn't disguise itself as living.

Having a plan is important. Your future will turn out completely unlike your plan, but as you keep readjusting your plan, you will be a partner to change instead of at its mercy.

One of the main reasons that a master grows and a novice stumbles is that the master is always unaffected by detractors.

As we walk to get the mail, we think about
how depressing some of the mail might be
and give no thought to the blessing that we are
able to walk to get the mail.

Almost all self-help can be reduced to the simple
fact that good thoughts strengthen us and negative
thoughts weaken us.

Your relatives and friends will not sit around and
praise your life for the good you had planned to do.

Remember that you always produce
justification for the way you feel, but that
doesn't mean you are right.

When someone does not acknowledge your kindness, it is the perfect time to find out if your kindness is motivated by your love or by their indebtedness.

If your plans are not working out, it may not be the fault of your planning. A plan merely launches a creation, but it is your attitude that sets its course.

What you learn today is not meant to be wasted on judging yesterday, but to prepare you for tomorrow.

People are often powerless when something out of the ordinary happens to them only because doing something out of the ordinary has become so foreign to them.

Most people will give advice to you for two reasons. The first reason is because they love you and they have felt the pain of their own mistakes. Listen to these people. The second reason that people give advice is because they feel superior to you in age or experience. When getting advice from the second group always ask yourself – does this person excel in that area of life?

Where is your advice coming from?

When you feel like you have come to a dead stop in your life, it's because you have walked right up to a turn in your path but have refused to turn with it.

When you lose, applauding the other team for an outstanding performance keeps you always focused on your victory.

The fool comes to a boulder, takes a strong stance and curses the boulder. The wise one acknowledges the boulder and finds a path around it.

When we look at the night sky, there is no dread because we focus on the light from the moon and stars and not the darkness around them.

Every single day of your life you have the ability to take at least the smallest step toward the fulfillment of your dream. Waiting for a great leap will insure that it only stays a dream.

Be honest and ask yourself, what would it take for me to love what I am doing? If the answer involves other people changing, it's the wrong answer.

In school you are given quizzes to ensure that you are keeping up with the material and able to pass the final. In life, you are given sickness and sadness for the same reason.

It is better to eat with an old wooden spoon and a smile then with a new golden fork and a frown.

If you are lucky, you will find a place of peace and quiet. If you are wise, you will create one.

When we are told to go inside to find the answers, the biggest mistake we make is going to the mind instead of the heart.

Self-criticism is a toxic byproduct of criticizing others.

The happiness award doesn't necessarily go to the person who figures it all out. It goes to the person that is okay with not knowing all of the answers.

If you wish to know which path to follow, the best guidance is to choose the one that causes some discomfort. The path that seems devoid of discomfort usually contains much more.

The fine art of selective forgetting is a necessary course to master if you are to be a friend to yourself or to anyone else.

Setting yourself up to be stern and strong above all else is a call that goes out to say, I am terrified of feeling lost.

Boredom is a clear sign that you have forgotten that you always feel uplifted when you are helping another.

One of the most beautiful paradoxes in life is the fact that you must actively seek in order to find out that you already have what you seek.

No matter how loud you yell a positive affirmation, the whisper of what you feel in your heart will still be louder.

The problem with finding yourself in polluted water is not which stroke to use, but how to get out. Some problems require an exit strategy not coping skills.

The three most important words in making your dreams a reality are: set a date. There is nothing like a deadline to spur us to unimagined creativity.

There are many entrances to negativity
but over the main entrance is the word criticize.

Most people's egos will be uplifted by their
successes, but everyone's character will always be
defined by how they handle their failures.

As you figure out the way in which
the world would be better,
your own life is passing by, unheeded.

When you decide to make some changes in your
life, they happen much faster if you don't stop to
make yourself or someone else wrong first.

The quest for perfection is just another desire dressed up in a regal robe. All desires are a childish effort to feel more satisfied with life.

The downside to being sensitive to signs and portents is that every little ache and pain will seem to be a sign of a worse malady.

If we seek change as a step to a higher level, we will be helped. But if we seek change just to escape, we will be held back until we complete the lesson.

To gossip and talk endlessly about trivial subjects and then wonder where the chatter in our mind comes from is amusing.

Nothing is holding you back except your perception of how things are. It is amazing how many doors are closed but how few are locked.

Free will has nothing to do with what happens to you. Free will is all about how you choose to react to what happens to you.

Sitting on a train and pushing against the seat in front of you to make the train go faster is a waste of your energy. Everything will take as long as it takes.

If the food you want is a couple of feet away, you go and get it. Why do we wait for our dreams to come to us?

It is in holding a bit of ourselves back for security
that we fail to leap far enough to succeed.

In a society that praises academic learning as the
pinnacle of intelligence, the door to creativity is
usually blocked by the fear of being thought a fool.

A man with one leg on fire and the other
encased in ice is doing quite well on average.

When a diet, whether vegetarian or macrobiotic or
whatever, become a dogma to which we cling and
gives rise to self-righteousness or judgmentalism, it
also become our bondage.

The very worst question that you can ask yourself is "what is wrong with me?". Your mind is the greatest search engine. You ask and you receive. You will be shown everything that ever seemed wrong in your life. With so much evidence flooding in, you will quickly be convinced that your life is predominately wrong. It won't be the truth. It will just be what you asked for. And it will loom large because it will exclude anything good about you. Under the circumstances, the very best question that you can ask yourself is:

How can I feel better?

We accumulate to have something to turn to should
unhappiness make an appearance. So unhappiness
knows to send loss before it.

It is our learned ability to charge straight
ahead that has us running into obstacles.
Watch the way a river flows around an obstacle
taking little bites until it's gone.

Serenity comes from sitting and pondering what we
owe to others for the miracles in our life. Agitation
comes from pondering what they owe us.

Of all the things that happen on this planet,
there is nothing like a bona fide crisis somewhere
else to give us permission not to deal with
our own problems.

Any person can stand adversity.
The true test is to give a person power.

As we grow older it is necessary to have glasses to
see as we once did. It is also necessary to have
enthusiasm to live as we once did.

Getting upset is not a failure on any level.
Getting upset and blaming it on someone else is.

Read uplifting stories and listen to uplifting music
and then, and only then, take a good look at your
life and make plans for the future.

Oh, how incredibly important the latest news is
until we get a toothache or stub a toe.

If you meditated,
you'd be OM by now.

The greatest fool is the person who believes that
cleverness is a substitute for sensitivity.

One of the paradoxes of life is that you have to
accumulate enough knowledge to find out that it is
wisdom and not knowledge that is important.

There is no finer trickery than when our ego dresses
up like our heart and spews forth advice. Only those
who live in their heart will notice the deception.

Constantly remarking about how you
have given something up is just another
subtle way of staying attached.

You jumped when you found no bridge and you
made it to the other side. Don't let the exhilaration
of making the jump blind you to what you wanted
to do once you got there.

When someone says "Thank You" and we
respond with "No problem" we are stating a fact.
When we respond with "You are welcome,"
we are honoring their gratitude.

Sometimes tears must leave our bodies
to make room for more courage.

How fast can you name your favorite person,
place, and song? How fast can you name your
worst pain, regret, and fear? The winner is the one
that shapes your life.

Our studies have fooled us into believing that it is
the knowledge of words and our ability to use them
that shows our greatness when it is our actions that
count for so much more.

All envy stems from the illusion that there is
someone else that is having an easier time than us.
The truth is that everyone, no matter who they are,
has a cross to bear.

The advance of age does not bring wisdom
by itself. It is the inevitable slowing down
with age that allows a life that was a blur
to slowly come into focus.

We were given an endless supply of kind words to
use and yet they seem so rare.

You will never know which of your words will be
held onto for a lifetime by someone else. Choose
wisely.

We become so good at juggling problems that we
forget to take the time to solve them.

The first law of conscious living is:
Just because someone agrees with you
doesn't meant that you are right.

When wrong finally changes to right,
right will seem wrong for a while.

Wisdom is most aptly demonstrated not by saying
wise words but by not saying harmful ones.

If you placed the radio dial between stations and
just left it there, it would be a great waste of an
appliance. If you allow your mind to remain
unfocused, it's a great waste of a life.

The biggest obstacle to our personal
growth is having found someone to
blame for our lack of progress.

If you did not change one thing in your room but
changed your thoughts, the room would change.

If we were to see the perfect wave or the
perfect rose, we would expect it to change as time
went by; and yet, we expect our lives to someday
be perfect and stay that way.

Yesterday was alive in what used to be present.
If you wish to keep yesterday alive, you must
borrow time from today but be aware that
you are using diamonds to buy rust.

Patience is the ability to be the
master of time rather than being its slave.

We remember so vividly the problems
of the past but remember so dimly the
strength that overcame them.

What flower in this whole world does not
bloom because the news is bad?

Passion in any area of life is our soul's proclamation
of being alive. Should passion fade, drama is always
ready to take its place.

Keys to living are many but even those without keys
or without even the knowledge of the existence of
keys manage to live quite well.

We curse that fact that everything
changes and then we sit in awe at the
evening colors of the sunset.

Most people don't want to be part of a crisis but
most people will find a way in conversation to link
themselves to a crisis that has happened.

When your last day on earth is over,
there will be tears. Whether they are tears of love
or tears of pity will depend upon what you
considered important in your life.

You don't have to push everyone away to prove that you can stand on your own soul.

Efficiency is a wonderful ability but without the addition of wisdom, you will never understand which things are worth doing slowly.

Looking in the mirror one day, we think how old. Looking back in the future at a photograph of that same day, we think how young.

Concentrate on helping yourself and you are flooded with thoughts. Concentrate on helping someone else and your thoughts quiet down.

We read and listen and try to find the words that will liberate us and yet both the rainbow and the rose say not a word.

You are not here to get better at dealing with people who push your buttons. You are here to inactivate those buttons.

There are those days when we feel a little off. Running through our mind like a crazed detective trying to find the cause, we forget that we can laugh and accept being a little off.

You don't have to find the right words or moment to speak up. You only have to find a time when your trust is more important than feeling uncomfortable.

If you slipped and fell into a hole, you would
not try to slip and fall out of it. If thinking a certain
way got you into trouble, thinking that same way is
unlikely to get you out.

If you run to the back of the boat to
study where you have been, you relinquish
every possibility of steering it.

There were those who stayed calm and
loving when you ranted and raved.
You owe it to them to be calm and loving
when someone else rants and raves.

Something that will be grand and wonderful
never appears at first glance to be grand and
wonderful. It just seems different.

Negativity doesn't care that you have locked it out of your thoughts. It waits until seriousness unlocks the door, cynicism opens the door, and then it just walks right in and takes over.

You may or may not be living your dreams but you are most certainly living your thoughts.

Be clear with your words and confusion may still follow. Be clear with your intent and the right words will always follow.

The first and most important lesson to master on the path of joy is that when something is wrong, it never, ever, means that everything is wrong.

As long as we wish for a police car to be there when someone runs a red light and wish for it not to be there when we do, there is work to be done.

The irony of a good education is that you have many important things to say but find it almost impossible to say I don't know.

Dreams are wonderful highlights of sleeping but if you want your dreams to come true, you must awaken.

Defend those who are weak or asleep, help where you can, live from your soul and be a pirate of Heaven.

You don't judge a game by the first
minutes or a book by the first words.
Save your judgment of your life until
you are sure it is over.

CPSIA information can be obtained
at www.ICGtesting.com
Printed in the USA
BVHW080941140620
581357BV00003B/88